I'm Thinking of a Zoo Animal

Bela Davis

Abdo Kids Junior
is an Imprint of Abdo Kids
abdobooks.com

Abdo
I'M THINKING OF AN ANIMAL
Kids

abdobooks.com

Published by Abdo Kids, a division of ABDO, P.O. Box 398166, Minneapolis, Minnesota 55439.

Printed in the United States of America, North Mankato, Minnesota.

052024

092024

THIS BOOK CONTAINS RECYCLED MATERIALS

Photo Credits: Getty Images, Shutterstock

Production Contributors: Teddy Borth, Jennie Forsberg, Grace Hansen

Design Contributors: Candice Keimig, Pakou Moua

Library of Congress Control Number: 2023948537

Publisher's Cataloging-in-Publication Data

Names: Davis, Bela, author.

Title: I'm thinking of a zoo animal / by Bela Davis

Description: Minneapolis, Minnesota : Abdo Kids, 2025 | Series: I'm thinking of an animal | Includes online resources and index.

Identifiers: ISBN 9798384900559 (lib. bdg.) | ISBN 9798384901259 (ebook) | ISBN 9798384901600 (Read-to-me eBook)

Subjects: LCSH: Zoo animals--Juvenile literature. | Questions and answers--Juvenile literature. | Riddles--Juvenile literature. | Animals--Juvenile literature. | Zoology--Juvenile literature.

Classification: DDC 636.08--dc23

Table of Contents

Guess the Animal! . . .4

Comparing Animals. 22

Glossary. 23

Index 24

Abdo Kids Code. 24

Guess the Animal!

I'm thinking of a zoo animal. Can you guess what it is?

DINO SAURS!
AT THE HOUSTON ZOO
NOW OPEN
ZOO
ENTRANCE

I'm thinking of an animal

that is strong.

clues

- strong

But it is not a kangaroo!

I'm thinking of an animal
that is big.

clues

- strong
- big

But it is not a moose!

I'm thinking of an animal that eats meat.

clues

- strong
- big
- eats meat

But it is not a shark!

I'm thinking of an animal that has four legs.

clues

- strong
- big
- eats meat
- has four legs

But it is not a crocodile!

I'm thinking of an animal that has **fur**.

clues

- strong
- big
- eats meat
- has four legs
- has fur

But it is not a wolf!

I'm thinking of an animal that can **climb** trees.

clues

- strong
- big
- eats meat
- has four legs
- has fur
- climbs trees

But it is not a leopard!

Do you know what animal I'm thinking of?

clues

- strong
- big
- eats meat
- has four legs
- has fur
- climbs trees

I'm thinking of a bear!

Now it's your turn! What animal are you thinking of?

Comparing Animals

	moose	crocodile	wolf	bear
strong	✓	✓	✓	✓
eats meat		✓	✓	✓
has fur	✓		✓	✓
climbs trees				✓

Glossary

climb
to go up, especially by using the feet and sometimes the hands.

fur
the soft thick hair that covers the bodies of certain animals.

Index

bear 20

climbing 16

crocodile 13

food 10

fur 14

kangaroo 7

legs 12

leopard 17

moose 9

shark 11

size 8

strength 6

wolf 15